The 11th Commandment

Commandment

Wisdom from Our Children

by The Children of America

I am the Lord your God.

You shall not take the name of the Lord

Keep holy

Honor your father and your mother.

You shall

You shall not steal.

You shall not bear false witn

You shall not covet yo

For information regarding permission to reprint material from this book,
please mail or fax your request in writing to Jewish Lights Publishing,
Permissions Department, at the address/fax
number listed below, or e-mail your request
to permissions@jewishlights.com.

Editor: Sandra Korinchak
Front cover art by Melek Erdinc
Back cover art by Lauren Tassos

Library of Congress Cataloging-in-Publication Data
The 11th commandment.
p.   cm.
Summary: American children's suggestions for an eleventh commandment,
illustrated with their drawings.
ISBN-13: 978-1-879045-46-0 (hc)
ISBN-10: 1-879045-46-X (hc)
1. Children—Conduct of life—Juvenile literature.
2. Children—Religious life—Juvenile literature.
3. Children's writings, American.
[1. Conduct of life. 2. Children's writings.]
BJ1631.A13 1995   95-38956
170'.44—dc20   CIP
                                        AC

Manufactured in the United States of America

For People of All Faiths, All Backgrounds
Jewish Lights Publishing
A Division of LongHill Partners, Inc.
An imprint of Turner Publishing Company
4507 Charlotte Avenue, Suite 100
Nashville, TN 37209
Tel: (615) 255-2665
www.jewishlights.com

You shall not cov

The 11

Introduction

"If there were an Eleventh Commandment, what would it be?"

We asked children from many different faiths and backgrounds to share their answers with us. Hundreds responded; and while their drawings and words come from many places, religions, and lifestyles, all come from the heart.

These commandments reveal the way our children hear God's voice in the world around them, their thoughts and concerns about life today, and their ideas about how people should respond to God.

Whether they come from the inner city, the suburbs or the country, a church or a synagogue, these commandments share the same clear message: In the ways we interact with our world—in our relationships with other people; with the earth; with family; with ourselves—we are interacting with God.

These "Eleventh Commandments" create a vivid image of the connections we share. They help all of us to see the world from a child's view...and, most importantly, they invite us to act on these visions to make our world a holy place.

Living with Other People

Living with the Earth

Living with Family

Living with Ourselves

Living with God

Living with Other People

love one another no matter who

Rebecca Lucas, 12, Bethany Birches Camp

thou shall be friends with everyone

Kristina Bosse, 11, Our Lady of Hope / St. Luke

Melek Erdinc, 11, Our Lady of Hope / St. Luke

no grabbing

Sarah Henschel, 5, Unitarian Church of All Souls

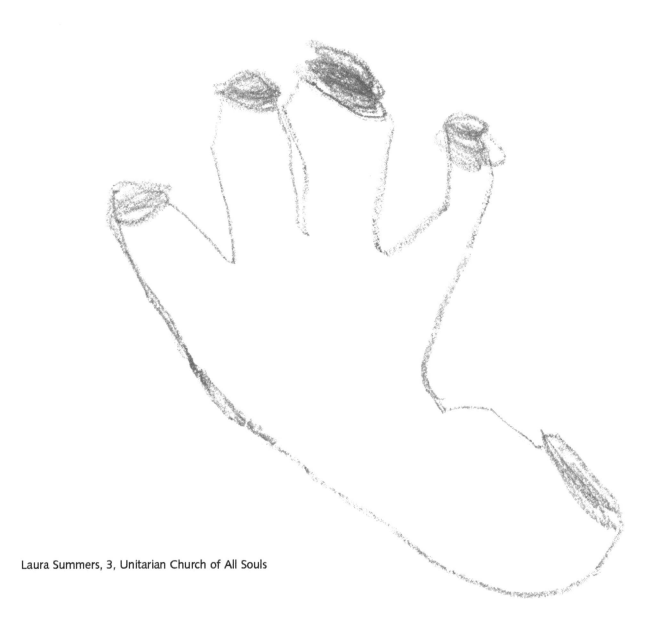

Laura Summers, 3, Unitarian Church of All Souls

do not choke other people

Brian Maher, 7, Central Baptist Church

don't judge someone by the color of their skin

Marsha Movshovich, 9, Central Synagogue

Veronica Powell, 10, Abyssinian Baptist Church

thou shall not have racism in thy mind or heart

Veronica Powell, 10, Abyssinian Baptist Church

be nice

Jireh Billings, 6, North Universalist Chapel

Jireh Billings, 6, North Universalist Chapel

no punching in the head

Carla Diaz, 4, Unitarian Church of All Souls

do not pick on people because of their race or if they're male or female

Elizabeth Hoffman, 9, Central Synagogue

Elizabeth Hoffman, 9, Central Synagogue

Jessie Burnham, 9, Central Baptist Church

do not be mean or stare at people with disabilities

Jessie Burnham, 9, Central Baptist Church

**you shall treat
men and women equally**

Justine Kahn, 11, Woodstock Area Jewish Community

**thou shall not
address people by their color**

Raven Dunbar, 9, Abyssinian Baptist Church

thou shall not judge your neighbor by their outside, nor shall you judge on the inside, for a wise person does not judge at all

Ashley Wetzel, 11, St. Agnes School

Elizabeth Wetmore, 9, North Universalist Chapel

feed everyone and eat together

Tommy Chester, 6, North Universalist Chapel

help the poor

Zach Schaffran, 9, Central Synagogue

Zach Schaffran, 9, Central Synagogue

you shall always try to help those in need

Ryan Meshulam, 11, Congregation Beth-El Zedeck

thou shall not hurt one another

Rachel Sands, 9, Catholic Community School

Katie Pryor, 6, Unitarian Church of All Souls

do not fight back

Andrew Kuo, 8, Fair Oaks Presbyterian Church

they shall not have hatred in them

Nicole Harrison, 9, Abyssinian Baptist Church

thou shall not shoot people

Liane Hunter, 7, Abyssinian Baptist Church

Emily Blair, 11, St. Agnes School

stop the violence !

Derrick Doles, 11, Mother Seton Academy

thou shall not create war at all

Rachel Stahm, 11, Our Lady of Hope / St. Luke

Daniel Whittington, 7, Fair Oaks Presbyterian Church

no bombing just for the heck of it

Daniel Whittington, 7, Fair Oaks Presbyterian Church

you shall not break other people's things on purpose

Raven Dunbar, 9, Abyssinian Baptist Church

Raven Dunbar, 9, Abyssinian Baptist Church

thou shall mediate...
when others are fighting

Natalie Beaty, 11, Our Lady of Hope / St. Luke

through sharing,
have peace with everyone

Robin Tiller, 9, North Universalist Chapel

Kim Proctor, 10, Catholic Community School

peace leads to friendship

Holly Nagel, 8, Fair Oaks Presbyterian Church

Living with the Earth

you shall take care of Mother Nature

Kelly O'Connell, 11, St. Agnes School

Ashley Neuhof, 7, North Universalist Chapel

Jennifer Lindner, 11, Our Lady of Hope / St. Luke

Isabel Oliveres, 4, Unitarian Church of All Souls

treat nature
with love and respect

Amy Lynn Comet, 9, Catholic Community School

be kind to animals

Donald Dougherty, 10, St. Jane Frances School

we shall not pollute the world

Steven Zappardino, 9, Our Lady of Pompei

Sludge-R-Us

Sean Ryan, 7, Sayville Congregational United Church of Christ

you shall not cut too much trees down

Angela Messina, 8, Woodstock Area Jewish Community

don't kill what you don't need

Emily Caroline Pease, 11, Bethany Birches Camp

Angela Messina, 8, Woodstock Area Jewish Community

plant a tree

Adam Koplewicz, 9, Central Synagogue

make more flowers for the world

Sarah Walstra, 6, Fair Oaks Presbyterian Church

Amy Lynn Comet, 9, Catholic Community School

you shall always have a family day

Kayla Wilson, 8, Catholic Community School

you must be nice to Mom

Chelsea Stetson, 6, North Universalist Chapel

Chelsea Stetson, 6, North Universalist Chapel

never take advantage
of your elders

Dorian Bryant, 11, Mother Seton Academy

thou shall not accuse others
for something you did

Meghan Brown, 11, St. Agnes School

Karen Briggs, 9, Catholic Community School

Liana Muskin, 9, Central Synagogue

Kelly Rupinski, 8, Catholic Community School

thou shall not speak with rudeness

Jennifer Saraullo, 11, St. Agnes School

Rebecca Lucas, 12, Bethany Birches Camp

try not to get divorced

Mary Cate Walker, 8, Fair Oaks Presbyterian Church

do not be frustrated
or else your anger
will wreck the beautiful
times with your family

Liana Muskin, 9, Central Synagogue

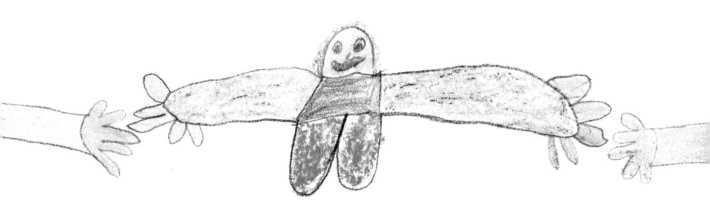

Bryan Tuckman, 6, Congregation Beth-El Zedeck

Living with ourself

you shall have belief and trust in yourself

Quiebonnie McDonald, 10, Mother Seton Academy

be a kid before you're an adult!
(you'll only be a kid once)

Christina Evans, 11, St. Jane Frances School

John Cermak, 11, St. Jane Frances School

you should play

Phebe Meyers, 6, North Universalist Chapel

mind your own business

Monica Powers, 11, Mother Seton Academy

Desmond Gray, 11, Mother Seton Academy

you must respect everything God has created, including your self

Dawn Clarke, 11, St. Agnes School

thou shall only do positive things to yourself and others

Scott McDowell, 11, St. Agnes School

Lauren Tassos, 7, St. Andrew the Apostle Byzantine Catholic Church

thou shall keep thy body safe

Katie Rothe, 11, St. Agnes School

do sports not drugs

Tony Soto, 9, Catholic Community School

Erin Lukas, 11, Catholic Community School

do not smoke

Spencer Doar, 7, Fair Oaks Presbyterian Church

thou shall not do anything you don't want to do (drugs, alcohol, gangs)

Akilah Speaks, 11, Mother Seton Academy

Scott McDowell, 11, St. Agnes School

thou shall keep your body healthy as in thou shall not pig out

Ali Dagger, 9, Woodstock Area Jewish Community

NAME: John   Date: 10/24/95

Subject: Spelling

speek	mouth	board	see
tork	lung	nail	saw
cork	bug	finger	pencil

1. cork   8. finger
2. bug   9. lung
3. mouth   10. tork
4. see   11. saw
5. nail   12. board
6. pencil
7. speek

NAME: Craig   Date: 10/24/95

Subject: Spelling

speek	mouth	board	see
tork	lung	nail	saw
cork	bug	finger	pencil

1. cork   8.
2. bug   9.
3.   10.
4.   11.
5.   12.
6.
7.

Garry Konig, 10, Catholic Community School

thou shall not cheat

Garry Konig, 10, Catholic Community School

Molly Bodner, 8, Congregation Beth-El Zedeck

fat, skinny, tall or thin, remember, God made you in his own image— the way he wanted you to be

Charlotte Ulle, 12, Bethany Birches Camp

Living with God

care, love, honor and respect God forever

Erin Littlejohn, 11, Our Lady of Hope / St. Luke

Bonnie Nugent, 11, St. Joseph's School

Bonnie Nugent, 11, St. Joseph's School

Laura Ward, 8, First United Methodist Church

follow the will of God

Veronica Delgado, 11, St. Joseph's School

Kelly Kay, 10, St. Jane Frances School

Lawrence McWatters, 10, Catholic Community School

Mario Soto, 10, Catholic Community School

Seth Orensky, 6, Central Baptist Church

Jennifer Kennedy, 11, St. Agnes School

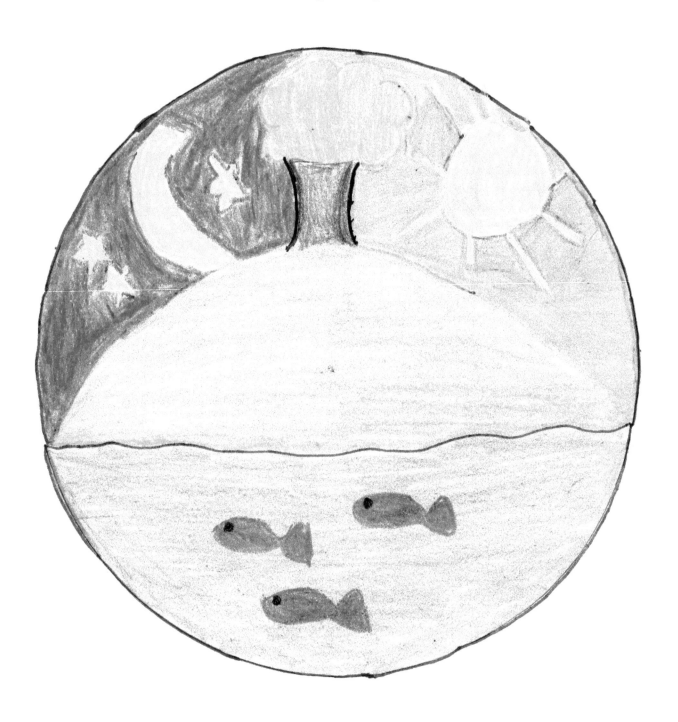

listen to God

Nora Pullen, 5, Central Baptist Church

About the Contributors

Abyssinian Baptist Church
(Baptist)
New York, NY

Bethany Birches Camp
(Mennonite/Interdenominational)
Plymouth, VT

Catholic Community School
(Roman Catholic)
Baltimore, MD

Central Baptist Church
(American Baptist Churches, USA)
Wayne, PA

Central Synagogue
(Reform)
New York, NY

Congregation Beth-El Zedeck
(Reconstructionist)
Indianapolis, IN

Fair Oaks Presbyterian Church
(Presbyterian)
Oak Park, IL

First United Methodist Church
(United Methodist)
Greeley, CO

Mother Seton Academy
(Interdenominational)
Baltimore, MD

North Universalist Chapel
(Unitarian Universalist)
Woodstock, VT

Our Lady of Hope / St. Luke
(Roman Catholic)
Baltimore, MD

Our Lady of Pompei
(Roman Catholic)
Baltimore, MD

St. Agnes School
(Roman Catholic)
Baltimore, MD

St. Andrew the Apostle Byzantine
Catholic Church
(Byzantine Catholic)
Gibsonia, PA

St. Jane Francis School
(Roman Catholic)
Pasadena, MD

St. Joseph's School
(Roman Catholic)
Cockeysville, MD

Sayville Congregational United
Church of Christ
(United Church of Christ)
Sayville, NY

Unitarian Church of All Souls
(Unitarian Universalist)
New York, NY

Woodstock Area Jewish Community
(Interdenominational)
Woodstock, VT

Living with Other People
Natalie Beaty, Jireh Billings, Emily Blair,
Kristina Bosse, Jessie Burnham,
Tommy Chester, Daniel Whittington,
Carla Diaz, Derrick Doles, Raven Dunbar,
Melek Erdinc, Nicole Harrison,
Sarah Henschel, Elizabeth Hoffman,
Liane Hunter, Justine Kahn, Andrew Kuo,
Rebecca Lucas, Brian Maher,
Ryan Meshulam, Marsha Movshovich,
Holly Nagel, Veronica Powell, Kim Proctor,
Katie Pryor, Rachel Sands, Zach Schaffran,
Rachel Stahm, Laura Summers, Robin Tiller,
Elizabeth Wetmore, Ashley Wetzel

Living with the Earth
Amy Lynn Comet, Donald Dougherty,
Adam Koplewicz, Jennifer Lindner,
Angela Messina, Ashley Neuhof,
Kelly O'Connell, Isabel Oliveres,
Emily Caroline Pease, Sean Ryan,
Sarah Walstra, Steven Zappardino

Living with Family
Karen Briggs, Meghan Brown,
Dorian Bryant, Rebecca Lucas,
Liana Muskin, Kelly Rupinski,
Jennifer Saraulio, Chelsea Stetson,
Bryan Tuckman, Mary Cate Walker,
Kayla Wilson

Living with Yourself
Molly Bodner, John Cermak, Dawn Clarke,
Ali Dagger, Spencer Doar, Christina Evans,
Desmond Gray, Garry Konig, Erin Lukas,
Quiebonnie McDonald, Scott McDowell,
Phebe Meyers, Monica Powers,
Katie Rothe, Tony Soto, Akilah Speaks,
Lauren Tassos, Charlotte Ulle

Living with God

If there were an Eleventh Commandment, what would it be?
Write and illustrate your answer on this page.

If there were an Eleventh Commandment, what would it be?
Write and illustrate your answer on this page.

Other Children's Books

Adam & Eve's First Sunset •AWARD WINNER•
God's New Day

by Sandy Eisenberg Sasso

Explores fear and hope, faith and gratitude, in a way that kids will understand.

For ages 4 & up. 32 pp, full-color illus., HC,
ISBN-13: 978-1-58023-177-0, ISBN-10: 1-58023-177-2, $17.95

Also available—a board book for kids 0–4:
Adam & Eve's New Day ISBN-13: 978-1-59473-205-8,
ISBN-10: 1-59473-205-1, $7.99

Because Nothing Looks Like God

by Lawrence and Karen Kushner

Shows how God is with us every day, in every way and helps introduce children to the possibilities of spiritual life. Real-life examples of happiness and sadness invite parents and children to explore, together, the questions we *all* have about God, no matter what our age.

For ages 4 and up. 11 x 8½, 32 pp, HC,
ISBN-13: 978-1-58023-092-6, ISBN-10: 1-58023-092-X, $16.95

Cain & Abel •AWARD WINNER•
Finding the Fruits of Peace

by Sandy Eisenberg Sasso

A beautiful recasting of the biblical tale. A spiritual conversation-starter about anger and how to deal with it, for parents and children to share.

Ages 5 & up. 32 pp, full-color illus., HC,
ISBN-13: 978-1-58023-123-7, ISBN-10: 1-58023-123-3, $16.95

For Heaven's Sake •AWARD WINNER•

by Sandy Eisenberg Sasso

Isaiah, a young boy, searches for heaven and learns that it is often found in the places where you least expect it.

For ages 4 & up. 32 pp, full-color illus., HC,
ISBN-13: 978-1-58023-054-4, ISBN-10: 1-58023-054-7, $16.95

God in Between •AWARD WINNER•

by Sandy Eisenberg Sasso

If you wanted to find God, where would you look? Teaches that God can be found where we are.

For ages 4 & up. 32 pp, full-color illus., HC,
ISBN-13: 978-1-879045-86-6, ISBN-10: 1-879045-86-9, $16.95

God Said Amen •AWARD WINNER•

by Sandy Eisenberg Sasso

A stubborn Prince and Princess show children and adults how self-centered actions affect the people around us, and how by working together we can work with God—to create a better world.

For ages 4 & up. 32 pp, full-color illus., HC,
ISBN-13: 978-1-58023-080-3, ISBN-10: 1-58023-080-6, $16.95

God's Paintbrush Celebration Kit
A Spiritual Activity Kit for Teachers and Students of All Faiths, All Backgrounds

by Sandy Eisenberg Sasso

With delightful illustrations and activity sheets to encourage discussion, this indispensable, completely nonsectarian teaching tool is designed for religious education settings in church and synagogue alike.

Five sessions for eight children ages 5–8.
40 full-color activity sheets and teacher folder,
ISBN-13: 978-1-58023-050-6, ISBN-10: 1-58023-050-4, $21.95

In God's Hands •AWARD WINNER•

by Lawrence Kushner and Gary Schmidt

Brings to life a traditional Jewish folktale, reminding parents and kids of all faiths and all backgrounds that each of us has the power to make the world a better place—working ordinary miracles with our everyday deeds.

For ages 5 and up. 9 x 12, 32 pp, HC,
ISBN-13: 978-1-58023-224-1, ISBN-10: 1-58023-224-8, $16.99

In Our Image •AWARD WINNER•
God's First Creatures

by Nancy Sohn Swartz

A playful new twist to the Genesis story, God asks all of nature to offer gifts to humankind—with a promise that the humans would care for creation in return.

For ages 4 and up. 9 x 12, 32 pp, HC,
ISBN-13: 978-1-879045-99-6, ISBN-10: 1-879045-99-0, $16.95

Noah's Wife •AWARD WINNER•
The Story of Naamah

by Sandy Eisenberg Sasso

A new story celebrating the wisdom of Naamah, whom God calls on to save each plant on earth in the Great Flood.

For ages 4 & up. 32 pp, full-color illus., HC,
ISBN-13: 978-1-58023-134-3, ISBN-10: 1-58023-134-9, $16.95

Also available—a board book version for ages 0–4:
Naamah, Noah's Wife ISBN-13: 978-1-893361-56-0,
ISBN-10: 1-893361-56-X, $7.95

9 781683 363583